The World of Plants

Flowers and Seeds

Carrie Branigan
and Richard Dunne

Smart Apple Media

First published in 2005 by Franklin Watts
96 Leonard Street, London EC2A 4XD

Franklin Watts Australia
45–51 Huntley Street, Alexandria NSW 2015

Editor: Rachel Cooke, Art director: Jonathan Hair, Designer: Michael Leaman
Design Partnership, Line illustrator: Jeremy Leaman, Picture researcher: Diana
Morris, Consultant: Gill Matthews

Picture credits:
Theo Allofs/Corbis: 25.
Mike Amphlett/Holt Studios: 11.
Nigel Cattlin/Holt Studios: front cover top, 3, 7b, 8t, 14t, 14b, 20, 21t, 23l, 24c, 26c.
Alan & Linda Detrick/Holt Studios: 10. Jurgen Dielenschneider/Holt Studios: 6.
Jack Fields/Corbis: 19br. Tim Fitzharris/Minden/FLPA: 12.
Garden World Images: 9, 15b, 18b, 22. Bob Gibbons/Holt Studios: 7t, 21b.
Jean Hall/Holt Studios: 24b. Gray Hardel/Corbis: 13t.
Roger Hosking/FLPA: 23r. Phili Marazzi/Ecoscene: 27c.
S&D&K Maslowski/FLPA: 13b. Rosie Mayer/Holt Studios: 15t.
Photowood Inc/Corbis: 8b. Robert Pickett/Ecoscene: 26r, 27cl, 27cr.
Inga Spence/Holt Studios: front cover below.

Published in the United States by Smart Apple Media
2140 Howard Drive West, North Mankato, Minnesota 56003

Library of Congress Cataloging-in-Publication Data

Branigan, Carrie.
Flowers and seeds / by Carrie Branigan and Richard Dunne.
p. cm. — (World of plants)
Includes index.
ISBN 1-58340-612-3
1. Flowers—Juvenile literature. 2. Seeds—Juvenile literature. 3. Botany—Juvenile literature.
I. Dunne, Richard. II. Title. III. Series.

QK49.B74 2005
575.6—dc22   2004065307

2 4 6 8 9 7 5 3 1

Contents

Flowers and Seeds

Most plants have **flowers**.

Flowers grow in many different colors, shapes, and sizes.

Flowers make a plant's **fruits** and **seeds**. The seeds are inside the fruits.

► This is a rose plant. Each flower forms a fruit called a rosehip. Inside the rosehip are the seeds.

flower

rosehip (seeds inside)

Flowers and the seeds they produce are very important. New plants grow from seeds.

◄ A new plant is growing from this seed.

Looking at Flowers

Flowers grow in different ways.

Some plants have one large flower.

▶ A daffodil has one large flower at the top of its **stem**.

Some plants have more than one flower.

◀ This tree has many flowers. Flowers that grow on trees are called **blossoms**.

Some plants have many small flowers held in a single flower head. These tiny flowers are called **florets**.

flower head

florets

petal

▲ The yellow center of each of these flower heads is made up of florets.

Most flowers have **petals**. Petals give the flower its shape and color.

Look at the different flowers on these two pages. What shape and color are their petals?

Moving Pollen

At the center of every flower are the parts that produce the plant's fruit.

Some of these parts make **pollen**. Pollen is a fine powder.

pollen

▲ You can see the yellow pollen at the center of this amaryllis flower.

Look at the center of different flowers. Can you see the pollen?

Pollen has to move from one flower to another for fruit to form. This is called **pollination**.

Some plants are **pollinated** by the wind.
The wind blows pollen from one flower
to another.

▲ A hazel bush is pollinated by the wind.
Its flowers are called catkins. Can you see
the pollen blowing out of them?

Animal Helpers

Some flowers are pollinated by animals. These animal helpers are usually insects.

Flowers pollinated by animals make a sugary drink called **nectar**. Many insects feed on nectar.

◀ When an insect drinks the nectar, pollen sticks to its body.

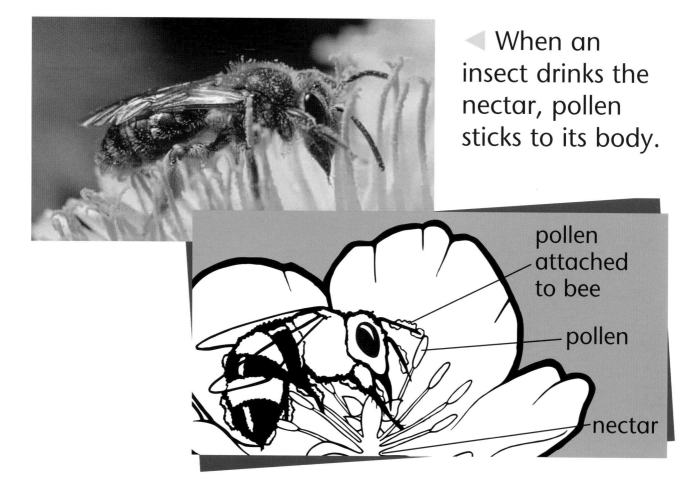

pollen attached to bee

pollen

nectar

Many flowers are brightly colored and smell sweet. How do you think this helps them to be pollinated?

When the insect goes to another flower to feed, the pollen on its body brushes off on that flower and pollinates it.

◁ Insects move pollen from flower to flower. After this happens, a flower can produce seeds.

In some parts of the world, birds and bats also pollinate flowers.

◁ The hummingbird has a long beak to reach the nectar in a flower.

Flower to Fruit

Once a flower is pollinated, the fruit begins to form.

▶ A bee pollinates an apple blossom.

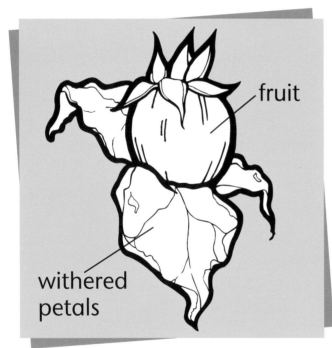

fruit

withered petals

▶ The fruit forms in the center of a flower. The petals fall off, leaving behind a small fruit.

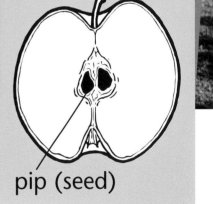

pip (seed)

▲ The fruit grows larger. The plant's seeds are inside.

Look at this picture of poppies. Which part of the flower do you think will become the fruit?

Inside a Fruit

Inside the fruit of a plant are its seeds. The fruit protects the seeds. Some fruits hold many seeds.

◀ If you cut open a melon, you will find hundreds of seeds inside.

seed

Some fruits have only a few seeds.

▶ Small seeds such as grape seeds are called **pips**.

pip

Some fruits have one seed called a **stone**.

stone

stone

▲ Peaches and avocados have stones.

All of the fruits on these two pages are soft and fleshy.

◀ A tomato is a soft fruit. We eat the fruit and the seeds inside.

seed

What fruits do you eat? How many seeds do they have inside them?

All Sorts of Fruit

There are many different kinds of fruits. Not all of them are soft and fleshy, but they all have seeds. Some seeds form in fruits called **pods**.

▶ Peas are seeds that grow in pods. What other seeds do we eat that come from pods?

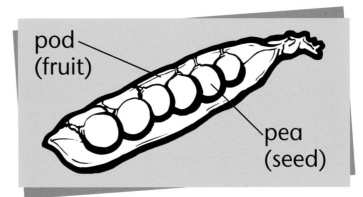

pod
(fruit)

pea
(seed)

Some fruits are hard and dry.

◀ An acorn is a dry fruit. Inside its hard shell is a softer seed.

Nuts are dry fruits. To eat them, we crack open the shells and eat the seeds inside. Do you like eating peanuts or hazelnuts?

With some plants, the fruits and the seeds cannot be separated. We call these plants **grains**.

◀ We eat rice and corn grains.

▼ We grind up wheat grains to make flour and then bread.

▲ We plant some grains to grow more food. Rice is planted in watery fields called paddy fields.

Scattering Seeds

To grow well, a seed needs to move away from the plant that made it. Plants scatter their seeds in different ways.

Some seeds are blown away by the wind.

◀ A dandelion is made up of tiny florets. Each one forms a seed with fluffy threads on its tip. The florets float away in the wind.

Have you ever blown on a dandelion? Try to find one the next time you go for a walk. What do the flying seeds remind you of?

Some pods dry out on the plant.
They then split open and scatter the
seeds inside them on the ground.

▲ When a lupin pod is dry, it opens, and
the seeds fall out.

Conkers are the seeds of horse chestnut trees.
They grow inside prickly fruits that split open
so the seed inside falls out.

Seeds and Animals

Many animals eat fruits and the seeds inside them. This helps plants spread their seeds.

▶ These mice are eating blackberries and the hard seeds inside them. After feeding, they will probably move away from the plant.

The seeds inside the fruits pass through the animals and come out in their droppings.

Birds eat fruit and seeds. Look for birds feeding when you go for a walk. What are they eating?

Some fruits are light and prickly.
They stick easily to an animal's fur
when it brushes past them.

▲ This is the prickly fruit of a burdock. It is called a **burr**.

▲ Burrs hook themselves to an animal's coat when it moves past them.

Later, the fruits fall off the animal, and the seeds inside can begin to grow.

Has a burr ever stuck to you, or to your cat or dog?

23

Waiting to Grow

Seeds may lie in the ground for a while. They need water and warmth to start to grow.

In parts of the world where winters are cold, seeds start to grow in the spring, when the weather gets warmer.

◄ A farmer planted this wheat in the winter. Now that it is spring, the wheat has started to grow.

▶ Some gardeners help seeds to grow by keeping them inside warm greenhouses.

Deserts get very little rain. The seeds of desert plants lie in the ground for a long time and grow very quickly after it rains.

▲ After a rainstorm in the Australian desert, plants grow and flower quickly to make more seeds.

Plant some seeds such as beans and place them on a sunny windowsill. Give some of them water. Keep some of them dry. Which ones start to grow?

Growing from a Seed

Inside every seed are the beginnings of a new plant. The plant is protected by the seed's case until it starts to grow.

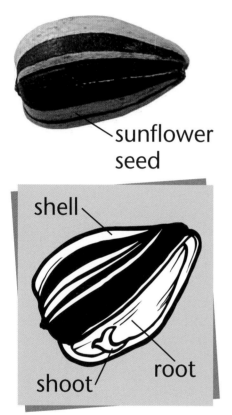

sunflower seed

shell

shoot

root

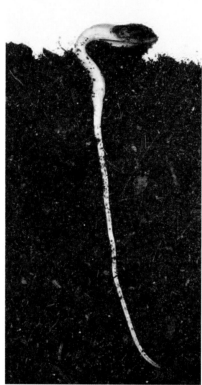

▲ Inside a seed is a **root** and a **shoot**. There is also food to give the new plant the energy it needs to start growing.

▲ First the root begins to grow down into the ground.

▲ Then the shoot pushes up above the ground and opens its **leaves**.

Soak some beans in water overnight. Then push them down the side of a glass jar filled with damp cotton balls. Put the jar somewhere sunny. Over the next week, watch as the root and the shoot start to grow.

▲ A plant makes food in its leaves. This gives it the energy to grow bigger and produce flowers.

▲ Insects visit the flower to feed on the nectar it makes. They pollinate the plant.

▲ The petals die. The plant has made its fruits and seeds, making it possible for more new plants to grow.

Amazing Facts

 The world's largest flower is the stinking corpse lily. It is found in Asia and measures about three feet (91 cm) across.

 A honeybee visits between 50 and 100 flowers on every trip it makes from its hive to collect nectar. Think how many flowers it helps pollinate during its lifetime!

The largest seed is the coconut. The double coconut, found in the Seychelles islands in the Indian Ocean, weighs 40 pounds (18 kg)—about as much as a small child.

Use this book to find the answers to this Amazing Plants quiz!

What is a floret?

How does pollen travel from one plant to another?

Once a flower has been pollinated, what happens to its petals?

How do we eat wheat grains?

Name three fruits that have stones inside them.

How do animals help plants by eating their fruit?

Is a pod a flower, a fruit, or a seed?

Glossary

blossoms flowers that grow on trees.

burr a type of prickly fruit that sticks to hair, fur, or clothing.

florets small flowers that are part of a bigger flower head.

flowers parts of a flowering plant that make its fruits and seeds.

fruits parts of a plant that grow from the flower and protect the seed or seeds.

grains seeds made by cereal plants such as wheat and rice.

leaves parts of a plant that use sunlight, air, and water to make food for the plant.

nectar a sugary liquid made in some flowers as food for insects and other animals. These animals pollinate the flowers as they move from plant to plant.

petals outer parts of a flower that are often colorful.

pips small, hard seeds found in some fruits.

pods types of fruit that grow on some plants, such as bean and pea plants.

pollen a fine powder made by flowers.

pollinated *see* **pollination**.

pollination the movement of pollen from one flower to another. Flowers need to be pollinated to make fruits and seeds. Pollen is moved from plant to plant by the wind or by animals.

root the part of a plant that holds the plant in the soil. Roots collect water from the soil.

seeds small parts made in the flower of a flowering plant. When seeds are planted, new plants grow from them.

shoot the first growth of a plant above the ground. It is usually made up of a stem and one or two leaves.

stem the part of a plant that holds up the leaves and flowers and connects them to the roots.

stone a large, single hard seed found in some fruits such as plums, peaches, and nectarines.

Index